Robert Aston

Hymns and verses on spiritual subjects

Being the sacred poetry of St. Alphonso Maria Liguori

Robert Aston

Hymns and verses on spiritual subjects
Being the sacred poetry of St. Alphonso Maria Liguori

ISBN/EAN: 9783742829382

Manufactured in Europe, USA, Canada, Australia, Japa

Cover: Foto ©Lupo / pixelio.de

Manufactured and distributed by brebook publishing software (www.brebook.com)

Robert Aston

Hymns and verses on spiritual subjects

THE SACRED POETRY

· OF

ST. ALPHONSO MARIA LIGUORI.

LONDON:
ROBSON AND LEVEY, PRINTERS, GREAT NEW STREET,
FETTER LANE.

Hymns and Verses on Spiritual Subjects:

BEING

THE SACRED POETRY

OF

ST. ALPHONSO MARIA LIGUORI,

FOUNDER OF THE CONGREGATION OF THE MOST HOLY REDEEMER.

TRANSLATED FROM THE ITALIAN,

AND EDITED BY

ROBERT A. COFFIN,

PRIEST OF THE CONGREGATION OF THE MOST HOLY REDEEMER.

LONDON:
BURNS AND LAMBERT, 17 AND 18 PORTMAN STREET,
AND 63 PATERNOSTER ROW.

NIHIL OBSTAT,

    Joan. Can. Poen. Morris,
        Rev. Syn.

Imprimatur.

    N. CARD. WISEMAN.

Westmon. 7 *Oct.* 1863.

TO ST. ALPHONSO.

A LIFE scarce stained by conscious sin,
Yet ever striving grace to win
With hair-shirt, fast, and discipline
    For crime reserved :—

An eye, which fourscore years and ten,
In lonely cell or haunts of men,
Fixed on God's Majesty a ken
    Which never swerved :—

A voice, whose every accent prayed;
A heart, which like a fountain played,
And falling heavenly music made
    In acts of love :—

A science, to which sages bow,
Which, though in simplest words it flow,
Now like the eagle soars, and now
    Wooes like the dove :—

A zeal, like Daniel's, quick to brave,
For God, the hungry lion's cave,
Yet opening wide its arms to save
    Poor fallen ones :—

If these can win a Seraph's crown,
Then, Saint Alphonso, 'tis thine own.
Ah! with a Seraph's love look down
    Upon thy sons!

NOTICE.

The present Translation is an humble attempt to render, as faithfully as possible, in our own language, the Sacred Poetry of St. Alphonso.

In order to attain this, it has been our endeavour to retain not only the ideas of the saintly Author, but even his forms of expression, and his very words, as far as was found practicable.

Having this object in view, it became a duty often to sacrifice style to exactness, and poetical form to a faithful reproduction of the original. In doing this, we have the consolation of believing that we are following in the steps of St. Alphonso himself, who was ever ready to abandon the highest literary excellence, for the sake of a single word which could lead to a greater love of Jesus and Mary.

The spirit of these compositions will not be thoroughly understood, unless the reader bears in mind, that they were for the most part written by St. Alphonso for the use of the people, and in order to replace the profane and dangerous love-songs, of which the Neapolitans were so passionately fond. He was accustomed, not only while yet a missionary, but even after his elevation to the episcopacy, to sing them himself before the people in the church, in order to animate them by his example. We learn from his biographer that, after the missions given by him, he had the consolation to see the fruit of his zealous endeavours in the general abolition of dangerous songs, which were replaced by his own DEVOTIONAL Hymns to Jesus and Mary.

As to the ASCETICAL and MYSTICAL poetry, which form a considerable portion of this collection, they must be regarded in the same light as the wonderful effusions of St. Teresa, St. John of the Cross, and other Saints, who were wont to give expression in verse to the uncontrollable ardours of Divine Love which consumed their hearts. We may therefore expect to find many sentiments which, unhappily, few will be able to make their own, and many perhaps will not even understand; but which ought to humble us all at the sight of our own coldness, and excite us to admire the effects of Divine Love in the saints, and to adore the mysteries of that Sacred Union which God deigns to contract, even here upon earth, with a faithful soul.

The Translation has been made for the most part from the Italian editions of the Saint's complete works, published at Monza and at Turin. A few pieces not to be found in those editions have been translated from a collection found in a Neapolitan edition printed during the lifetime of the Saint, in 1769, which was used by the Sacred Congregation in the examination of his works previous to his beatification, and is now preserved in the Archives of our Congregation in Rome. The "Ode on the Birth of our Lord," and the "Invocation of Mary in time of Temptation," have been translated from Mss. preserved likewise in the same Archives. Two others, Nos. 12 and 18, are taken from a Neapolitan Collection of Mission Hymns, and are attributed to the Saint.

May this little volume contribute not only to make St. Alphonso more known and appreciated, but also to increase amongst us that simplicity and tenderness of devotion which are the pervading characteristics of his spiritual writings, and which it was the aim of his life to instil into the hearts of all!

ROBERT ASTON COFFIN, C.SS.R.

St. Mary's, Clapham,
 Feast of the Assumption 1863.

CONTENTS.

Part I. DEVOTIONAL.

§ 1. OUR LORD JESUS CHRIST.

NO.		PAGE
1.	On the Birth of our Saviour Jesus Christ	1
	When Jesus first appeared on earth.	
2.	To the Infant Jesus in the Crib	11
	Oh, how I love Thee, Lord of Heaven above!	
3.	To the Infant Jesus	12
	O King of Heaven! from starry throne descending.	
4.	Hymn of St. Joseph, who addresses the Divine Child Jesus	13
	Since Thou the name of Father hast bestow'd.	
5.	On the Sacred Heart of Jesus	15
	I dwell a captive in this heart.	
6.	To Jesus in His Passion	17
	My Jesus! say, what wretch has dared.	
7.	To the Instruments of the Passion of Jesus	19
	O ruthless scourges, with what pain you tear.	
8.	To Jesus in the Tabernacle	20
	O flowers, O happy flowers.	
9.	For Holy Communion	23
	My soul, what dost thou!	
10.	To Jesus, after Communion	24
	O Bread of Heaven! beneath this veil.	

CONTENTS.

NO		PAGE
11.	Visit to Jesus on the Altar	27
	When the loving Shepherd.	
12.	Visit to the Blessed Sacrament . . .	30
	In this sweet Sacrament, to Thee.	

§ 2. THE BLESSED VIRGIN MARY.

13.	Mary our Hope	31
	Mary, thou art Hope the brightest.	
14.	Virgin of virgins	33
	Of all virgins thou art fairest.	
15.	Aspirations to Mary	35
	Knowest thou, sweet Mary.	
16.	Our Mother Mary	36
	Thou art clement, thou art chaste.	
17.	Mary, the Mother of Mercy	37
	Look down, O Mother Mary!	
18.	The Name of Mary	39
	Mother Mary, Queen most sweet.	
19.	On the Loveliness of Mary	41
	Raise your voices, vales and mountains.	
20.	A Soul the Lover of Mary	42
	I am the lover of a Queen.	
21.	The Madonna's Lullaby	44
	Mary sings, the ravish'd heavens.	
22.	The Mother of Sorrows	46
	O ye who pass along the way.	
23.	The Death of Mary	49
	Uplift the voice and sing.	

CONTENTS. xiii

NO.   PAGE

24. The Assumption of Mary 52
     Fly, my soul, with Mary fly!
25. Invocation of the Blessed Virgin . . . 54
     Haste, my Mother, run to help me.

Part II. ASCETICAL.

26. On the Tomb of Alexander the Great . 56
     Behold the end of all the pomp of earth.
27. Eternal Maxims 57
     Why serve the world, thy enemy?
28. Stanzas for the Evening Exhortations . 59
     'Tis the Lord hath sent me hither.
29. Act of Contrition 62
     I have offended Thee, my God.
30. Invitation to Solitude 63
     Fly hither, from the storm that rages round.
31. To the Holy Ghost. The Soul all for God 64
     Begone, ye vain hopes.
32. The Soul gives itself to Jesus 66
     World, thou art no more for me.
33. How amiable is the will of God . . . 68
     'Tis Thy good pleasure, not my own.
34. On the Love which Jesus bears to the Soul 70
     Oh! it were joy and high reward.

CONTENTS.

NO.   PAGE

35. Hymn to God the Creator 73
      Why didst Thou not create my soul.
36. The Soul sighing for God 74
      This heart of mine is sighing.
37. The Soul sighing for Heaven 76
      Oh! I am dying of desire.

Part III. MYSTICAL.

38. The Soul enamoured of the Beauty of God 78
      Let those who will for other beauties pine.
39. The Life of a Spouse 80
      To love is the only true life of a spouse.
40. Aspirations to Jesus 86
      Jesus, my sweetest Lord!
41. Dialogue between Jesus and the loving Soul 88
      Open to me, my sister.
42. The Soul inebriated with Divine Love . 103
      Oh! where am I!
43. The loving Soul in Desolation 108
      O dark and solitary grove.
44. In honour of St. Teresa 112
      Ye angels, most inflamed.
45. On the Words of St. Aloysius 114
      Poor heart, what art thou doing? say.

APPENDIX.

The subjoined hymns are inserted among the poetry of St. Alphonso in both the Turin and Monza editions of his works, but were not composed by the Saint.

NO.   PAGE

46. On the Sacred Heart of Jesus (Anonym.) 117
      Fly, my soul, ah, fly away.
47. On the Love of God (Mgr. Falcoja) . . 118
      O God of loveliness!
48. Mary our Mother (Mgr. Majello) . . . 122
      When I think o'er my happy lot.
49. To Mary assumed into Heaven (Mgr. Majello) 124
      Mary, thy heart for love.

Part First.

DEVOTIONAL.

§ 1. OUR LORD JESUS CHRIST.

---

1. *Ode on the Birth of Our Saviour Jesus Christ.*

WHEN Jesus first appeared on earth
    A babe in Bethlehem,
The winter midnight of His birth
    Did fair as noontide seem;
        Ne'er shone the stars so bright
        As on that wondrous night:
Swift to the East the brightest of them all
Darts through the sky, the Magi kings to call.

Awaken'd by th' unwonted light,
    The startled songster birds
Broke the lone stillness of the night
    With songs like angels' words;
        While chirping in the field,
        The grasshoppers revealed

The joy of earth: "Jesus is born!" they cried;
"Our God is born!" the warbling birds replied.

Fresh, as when washed by summer showers,
    Now bud the roses sweet;
And thousand, thousand fragrant flowers
    The Infant Saviour greet;
        While e'en the arid hay
        That in the manger lay
Decked out with leaf and bloom the poor abode,
And kissed the infant members of its God.

In fair Engaddi's flowery clime
    Now blooms the fragrant vine,
And ripening grapes, ere nature's time,
    In purple clusters twine.
        Sweet Babe! divinely fair!
        Thou art Love's cluster rare!
Coolness to burning lips Thou dost impart,
And warmth of love divine to frozen heart.

Now gentle peace reigned far and wide,
    In joy and liberty;
The sheep and lion side by side
    Were pastured happily;

The kid, with frolic gay,
　　Near tiger fierce can play,
And ox with savage bear secure from harm,
And lambkin near the wolf without alarm.

Joy, too, awoke at Jesus' birth,
　　And roamed creation free,
In heaven, in every tribe of earth,
　　O'er every land and sea;
　　　　And many a sleeper smiled
　　　　As when a little child,
And felt his heart rebounding in his breast,
While dreams of gladness mingled with his rest.

The watchful shepherds kept by night
　　The flocks of Bethlehem,
When lo! an Angel clothed in light
　　Appeared, and said to them,
　　　　" Good shepherds! do not fear,
　　　　Our gladsome tidings hear;
For peace and joy upon the world arise,
And sinful earth becomes a paradise!

To you this day in Bethlehem
　　A Saviour-King is born;

The Long-expected,—to redeem
   And save a world forlorn.
      Then haste, and you will find
      The Saviour of mankind,
An infant, swathed, and lying in a stall,
Amongst the poor, the poorest one of all."

The angel choirs in glittering throng
   From heaven to earth descend,
And in one sweet melodious song
   Their countless voices blend.
      " Glory to God above!
      Born is the King of Love!
Peace be, on earth, to men who have good will;
Let grateful concerts earth and heaven fill!"

Each shepherd's heart within his breast
   Bounded, with love inflamed,
And eagerly unto the rest
   His ardour thus proclaimed:
      " Why longer thus delay?
      Come, haste, away, away!
For ah! I languish with desire untold
My Infant God and Saviour to behold!"

The shepherds o'er the hill-top hie,
　　Like herd of startled deer;
With joy they soon the cave descry,
　　And to the crib draw near;
　　　　They see that Infant sweet,
　　　　With Mary at His feet,
And looks of love all beaming from His eyes
Appear like rays of bliss from Paradise.

Astonished, raptured, and enchained,
　　At this great sight they saw,
Long time the shepherds thus remained
　　In solemn silent awe;
　　　　Then sweet and loving sighs
　　　　Deep from their hearts arise,
While mingled tears and words their love confess,
And in a thousand fervent acts express.

Then entering the poor abode,
　　With knees devoutly bent,
They humbly to the Infant God
　　Their simple gifts present;
　　　　And Jesus does not scorn
　　　　The poor and lowly-born,

But raising up to them His tiny hand,
He smiles a blessing on this humble band.

Then do the flames of heavenly fire,
    Which in their bosoms glow,
Such tender confidence inspire
    As love alone can know :
        They venture to embrace
        That Child of heavenly grace,
And on His hands and feet,—O happiness!—
A thousand times their fervent lips they press.

Then in their pipes these joyful swains
    Such heavenly music breathed,
And rivalling angelic strains,
    With tuneful Mary wreathed
        In sweetest harmony
        Such soothing lullaby,
That slumber o'er the infant eyelids crept,
And Jesus closed His lovely eyes, and slept.

The lullaby these shepherds blest
    To Jesus sung was this ;
Which gently, softly, lulled to rest
    The Infant God of bliss.

But while I now repeat
This cradle-song so sweet,
Think that with them beside the crib you kneel,
And pray the ardours of their love to feel.

" Gentle slumber, from above,
    Hush to sleep your heavenly King,
Born an Infant for our love!
    Hasten, sleep, soft slumbers bring!

Lovely Jewel of my heart!
    Would that I could be the sleep,
Softly, sweetly, to impart
    Closing eyes and slumbers deep.

But, if love of men to gain,
    Thus a babe Thou deign'st to be,
Love alone can sing the strain,
    Which can slumbers bring to Thee!

Since, then, love has power on Thee,
    Lo! my heart and soul are Thine!
Yes! I love Thee, love—but see!—
    Sleep has closed those eyes divine.

Thee, my God, alone I love!
　　Treasure! Beauty! Love, I . . . .
•　　•　　•　　•　　•
　　•　　•　　•　　•　　•"

Then breaking off their loving strain,
　All happy and content,
They hastened to their flocks again,
　　Rejoicing as they went;
　　　But such a heavenly fire,
　　　So ardent a desire
Of this dear Infant in their bosoms burns,
That to their thoughts He evermore returns.

In hell alone, where mortal hate,
　Despair, and terror dwell,
And in the hearts as obstinate
　　As demons loosed from hell,
　　　The splendours of that night
　　　Awakened strange affright;
Hardened in guilt, they trembled with dismay;
They hate the light which shows to heaven the
　　　　way.

Jesus! Thou art a Sun of Love,
    Whence beams of mercy dart;
Thy rays enlighten from above,
    And warm the sinner's heart.
        Though black and hard his soul,
        As changed to earthy coal,
Yet if repentant once he turns to Thee,
Thou show'st still more Thy loving clemency.

But, sweetest Child, ah! Jesus, say,
    Why flow those infant tears?—
Yes, 'tis that I may wash away
    My sins of bygone years!
        Alas! what have I done?
        Unkind, ungrateful one!
I sinned, I sinned, yet still Thou lovedst me:
Would I had died ere I offended Thee!

Oh! for a fountain flowing o'er
    With tears both night and day,
My sins unnumbered to deplore,
    And weep them all away!
        To bathe my Infant's feet,
        And by my sobs entreat

His mercy; then, oh! grant me once to hear
The word " *Thou art forgiven ; do not fear !*"

Thrice blest, thrice happy should I be
   With this too favoured lot!
All else on earth would seem to me
   Not worth one care, one thought.
     Thou Hope of the distress'd,
     Hear, Mary, my request!
Cease not to pray for this poor sinful one,
Who asks to love once more thy Blessed Son!

2. To the Infant Jesus in the Crib.

Oh, how I love Thee, Lord of Heaven above!
Too well hast Thou deserved to gain my love;
Sweet Jesus, I would die for love of Thee,
For Thou didst not disdain to die for me.

I leave thee, faithless world, farewell! depart;
This lovely Babe has loved and won my heart.
I love Thee, loving God, who from above
Didst come on earth, a Babe, to gain my love.

Thou tremblest, darling Child, and yet I see
Thy heart is all on fire with love for me:
Love makes Thee thus a child, my Saviour dear,
Love only brought Thee down to suffer here.

Love conquered Thee, great God, love tied
        Thy hands,
A captive here for me, in swathing bands;
And love, strong love, awaits Thy latest breath,
To make Thee die for me a cruel death.

3. To the Infant Jesus.

O King of Heaven! from starry throne descending,
    Thou takest refuge in that wretched cave;
O God of Bliss! I see Thee cold and trembling,
    What pain it cost Thee fallen man to save!

Thou, of a thousand worlds the great Creator,
    Dost now the pain of cold and want endure;
Thy poverty but makes Thee more endearing,
    For well I know 'tis love has made Thee poor.

I see Thee leave thy Heavenly Father's bosom,
    But whither has Thy love transported Thee?
Upon a little straw I see Thee lying;
    Why suffer thus? 'Tis all for love of me.

But if it is Thy will for me to suffer,
    And by these sufferings my heart to move,
Wherefore, my Jesus, do I see Thee weeping?
    'Tis not for pain Thou weepest, but for love.

Thou weepest thus to see me so ungrateful;
　　My sins have pierced Thee to the very core;
I once despised Thy love, but now I love Thee,
　　I love but Thee; then, Jesus, weep no more.

Thou sleepest, Lord, but Thy heart ever watches,
　　No slumber can a heart so loving take;
But tell me, darling Babe, of what Thou thinkest.
　　" I think," He says, " of dying for thy sake."

Is it for me that Thou dost think of dying?
　　What, then, O Jesus! can I but love Thee!
Mary, my hope! if I love Him too little,
　　Be not indignant; love Him, thou, for me.

―――

4. *Hymn of St. Joseph, who addresses the Divine Child Jesus.*

SINCE Thou the name of Father hast bestow'd
　　On me, my Jesus, let me call Thee Son.
My Son! I love—I love Thee; yes, my God!
　　For ever will I love Thee, dearest One!

Thou art my God! I humbly Thee adore;
  But, as my Son, ah! bid me kiss Thy face,
And make my heart remain for evermore
  Close bound with sweetest chains in Thy
    embrace!

Since Thou hast deigned to choose me here
    below,
  The nurse and guardian of Thy life to be,
My sweetest Love! my Good! ah! let me know
  What willest Thou?—what dost Thou ask
    of me?

All, all I am, to Thee I now resign;
  My love I consecrate to Thee alone;
And know, my heart is mine no more—'tis
    Thine;
  My very life I do not call my own.

Since Thou art pleased to share my humble
    home,
  And be on earth companion of my love,
Well may I hope, dear Jesus, to become
  Thy lov'd companion in Thy home above.

5. *On the Sacred Heart of Jesus.*

I DWELL a captive in this Heart,
   On fire with love divine;
'Tis here I live alone in peace,
   And constant joy is mine.

It is the Heart of God's own Son,
   In His Humanity,
Who, all enamoured of my soul,
   Here burns with love of me.

Here, like the dove within the Ark,
   Securely I repose;
Since now the Lord is my defence,
   I fear no earthly foes.

Now I have found this happy home,
   God's love alone I prize;
All else is torment to my heart,
   The world I now despise.

What though I suffer, still in love
   I ever true will be;
My love of God shall deeper grow
   When crosses fall on me.

Then he who longs with me to seek
  Repose within this nest,
All love that is not love for God
  Must banish from his breast.

Ye haughty lovers of the world,
  Full of self-love, depart!
Away, away! no place is found
  For you within this heart.

Each vile and earthly chain impedes
  The soul's true heavenward flight;
All, all the heart belongs to God,
  Love claims His sovereign right.

From ev'ry bond of earth, dear Lord,
  Thy grace has set me free;
My soul, delivered from the snare,
  Enjoys true liberty.

I cannot love Thee as I ought,—
  This pains me, this alone;
For all my love must have an end;
  Thy goodness, Lord, has none.

One thought brings comfort to my heart,—
   I love a God so great,
That though I love Him all I can,
   More love He merits yet.

Nought more can I desire than this,
   To see His face in heaven;
And this I hope, since He on earth
   His Heart in pledge has given.

---

6.   To Jesus in His Passion.

My Jesus! say, what wretch has dared
   Thy sacred hands to bind?
And who has dared to buffet so
   Thy face so meek and kind?
'Tis I have thus ungrateful been:
   Yet, Jesus, pity take;
Oh, spare and pardon me, my Lord,
   For Thy sweet mercy's sake!

My Jesus! who with spittle vile
   Profaned Thy sacred brow?

And whose unpitying scourge has made
    Thy precious blood to flow?
'Tis I have thus ungrateful been, &c.

My Jesus! whose the hands that wove
    That cruel thorny crown?
Who made that hard and heavy cross
    Which weighs Thy shoulders down?
'Tis I have thus ungrateful been, &c.

My Jesus! who has mocked Thy thirst
    With vinegar and gall?
Who held the nails that pierced Thy hands,
    And made the hammer fall?
'Tis I have thus ungrateful been, &c.

My Jesus! say who dared to nail
    Those tender feet of Thine?
And whose the arm that raised the lance
    To pierce that heart divine?
'Tis I have thus ungrateful been, &c.

And, Mary, who has murdered thus
    Thy loved and only One?
Canst thou forgive the blood-stained hand
    That robbed thee of thy Son?

'Tis I have thus ungrateful been
  To Jesus and to thee;
Forgive me for thy Jesus' sake,
  And pray to Him for me.

---

7.   To the Instruments of the Passion of Jesus.

O RUTHLESS scourges, with what pain you tear
My Saviour's flesh, so innocent and fair!
Oh, cease to rend that flesh divine,
  My loving Lord torment no more;
Wound rather, wound this heart of mine,
  The guilty cause of all He bore.

Ye cruel thorns, in mocking wreath entwin'd,
My Saviour's brow in agony to bind,
Oh, cease to rend that flesh divine,
  My loving Lord torment no more;
Wound rather, wound this heart of mine,
  The guilty cause of all He bore.

Unpitying nails, whose points, with anguish

Oh, cease to rend that flesh divine,
  My loving Lord torment no more;
Wound rather, wound this heart of mine,
  The guilty cause of all He bore.

Unfeeling lance, that dar'st to open wide
The sacred temple of my Saviour's side!
Oh, cease to wound that flesh divine,
  My loving Lord insult no more;
Pierce rather, pierce this heart of mine,
  The guilty cause of all He bore.

---

8. *Jesus in the Blessed Sacrament enclosed in the Tabernacle.*

O FLOWERS, O happy flowers, which day and
    night
  So near to my own Jesus silent stay,
And never leave Him, till before His sight
  At length your life in fragrance fades away!

Could I, too, always make my dwelling-place
    In that dear spot to which your charms you lend,
Oh, what a blessed lot were mine! what grace,
    Close to my truest Life, my life to end!

O lights! O happy lights, which burn away,
    The presence of our Jesus to proclaim,
Ah! could I see my heart become one day
    Like you, all fire of love and burning flame,
Then, as you waste away, so would I die,
    Like you, consumed with fire of love divine;
Oh! how I envy you! How blest were I
    Could I but change your happy lot with mine!

O sacred pyx! thou art more favoured still,
    For thou my love concealed dost here enclose;
What nobler, happier part could creature fill?
    In thee thy very God deigns to repose!
Ah! were thy office but for one brief day
    On this my poor and frozen breast bestow'd,
Then would my heart be melted all away,
    Of love and fire become the blest abode!

But ah, sweet flowers, bright lights, and pyx
    so blest!
Far, far more fortunate than you am I,
When my Belovèd comes within my breast,
    All loving like a tender lamb to lie;
And I, poor worm, in this frail host receive
    My Good, my All, the God of Majesty!
Why then not burn? my life why then not give,
    Since here my Treasure gives Himself to
    me?

Away, like fluttering moth around the light,
    My raptured soul, about thy Jesus fly,
Inflamed with faith and love; and at the sight
    Of thy Belovèd ever burn and sigh!
And when the hour arrives, and He is thine
    Whose very sight makes Paradise above,
Oh, press Him to thy heart with fire divine,
    And say thou wilt but love, love, only love!

9. *For Holy Communion.*

My soul, what dost thou? Answer me—
  Love God who loves thee well:—
Love only does He ask of thee,
  Canst thou His love repel?

See, how on earth for love of thee,
  In lowly form of bread,
The Sovereign Good and Majesty
  His dwelling-place has made.

He bids thee now His friendship prove,
  And at His table eat;
To share the bread of life and love,
  His own true flesh thy meat.

What other gift so great, so high,
  Could God Himself impart?
Could love divine do more to buy
  The love of thy poor heart?

Though once, in agonies of pain,
  Upon the cross He died,
A love so great, not even then
  Was wholly satisfied.

Not till the hour when He had found
    The sweet mysterious way
To join His heart in closest bond
    To thy poor heart of clay.

How, then, amid such ardent flame,
    My soul, dost thou not burn?
Canst thou refuse, for very shame,
    A loving heart's return?

Then yield thy heart, at length, to love
    That God of Charity,
Who gives His very self to prove
    The love He bears to thee.

---

10.   Hymn to Jesus after Communion.

O BREAD OF HEAVEN! beneath this veil
    Thou dost my very God conceal;
My Jesus, dearest Treasure, hail!
    I love Thee, and adoring kneel:
The loving soul by Thee is fed
With Thy own self in form of bread!

O Food of Life! Thou who dost give
    The pledge of immortality!
I live;—no, 'tis not I that live,
    God gives me life, God lives in me:
He feeds my soul, He guides my ways,
And every grief with joy repays.

O Bond of Love! that dost unite
    The servant to his loving Lord!
Could I dare live, and not requite
    Such love,—then death were meet reward:
I cannot live, unless to prove
Some love for such unmeasured love.

O mighty Fire! Thou that dost burn
    To kindle every mind and heart!
For Thee my frozen soul doth yearn;
    Come, Lord of Love, Thy warmth impart.
If thus to speak too bold appear,
'Tis love like Thine has banished fear.

O sweetest Dart of Love Divine!
    If I have sinned, then vengeance take:
Come, pierce this guilty heart of mine,
    And let it die for His dear sake

Who once expired on Calvary,
His Heart pierced through for love of me.

My dearest Good! who dost so bind
    My heart with countless chains to Thee!
O sweetest Love, my soul shall find
    In Thy dear bonds true liberty.
Thyself Thou hast bestowed on me,
Thine, Thine for ever I will be!

Belovèd Lord! in Heaven above,—
    There, Jesus, Thou awaitest me
To gaze on Thee with changeless love.
    Yes, thus I hope,—thus shall it be:
For how can He deny me heaven,
Who here on earth Himself hath given?

11. *The Visit to Jesus on the Altar.*

When the loving Shepherd,
   Ere He left the earth,
Shed, to pay our ransom,
   Blood of priceless worth,—
These His lambs so cherish'd,
   Purchased for His own,
He would not abandon
   In the world alone.

Ere He makes us partners
   Of His realm on high,
Happy and immortal
   With Him in the sky,—
Love immense, stupendous,
   Makes Him here below
Partner of our exile
   In this world of woe.

Lest one heart that loves Him
   E'er should sigh with pain,
Pining for His presence,
   Seeking Him in vain,—

DEVOTIONAL.

He on earth would tarry
    Near to every one,
That each heart might find Him
    On His altar-throne.

Yes, upon that altar,
    Captive in His cell,
Burning with affection,
    Jesus deigns to dwell.
Thence He seeks to kindle
    With His heavenly fires
Every heart that truly
    To His love aspires.

How that fire enkindles,
    Piercing like a dart,
He alone is witness
    Who has felt its smart:
Though the heart approaches
    Cold as falling snow,
Soon it melts and kindles
    From the furnace glow.

Say, ye souls enamour'd,
    What blest flames you feel;

OUR LORD JESUS CHRIST.

Say, what fiery arrows
    Pierce you as you kneel,
When you come to worship
    Where your Jesus lies,
All your love awaiting,
    Hid from mortal eyes.

Jesus, food of angels!
    Monarch of the heart,
Oh, that I could never
    From Thy face depart!
Yes, Thou ever dwellest
    Here for love of me,
Hidden Thou remainest,
    God of Majesty!

Soon I hope to see Thee,
    And enjoy Thy love,
Face to face, sweet Jesus,
    In Thy heaven above.
But on earth an exile,
    My delight shall be
Ever to be near Thee,
    Veiled for love of me.

12. *Verses to be sung by the People after the Visit to the Blessed Sacrament.*

In this sweet Sacrament, to Thee,
    My God, be ceaseless praise!
And to the name of Jesus be
    All love through endless days!

And blessèd too be Mary's womb,
    Which gave to us that Son,
More pure, more fair than lily-bloom,
    Jesus, the Blessed One.

Come now, my loving Lord, to me,
    Oh, come into my heart;
Inflame it all with love of Thee,
    And never thence depart.

And let this wretched heart be Thine,
    Yes, Thine, dear God, alone!
And, Mary, may this soul of mine
    Henceforth be all thy own!

§ 2. THE BLESSED VIRGIN MARY.

13. *Mary, our Hope.*

Mary, thou art Hope the brightest,
    Love most pure and sweet;
Life and peace I find, reposing
    At Thy blessed feet!

When I call on thee, O Mary,
    When I think on thee,
Joy and pleasure all-entrancing
    Fill my heart with glee.

If anon the clouds of sadness
    Rise within my heart,
When they hear thy name, O Mary,
    Straightway they depart.

Like a star on life's dark ocean,
    Shining o'er the wave,
Thou canst guide my bark to harbour,
    Thou my soul canst save.

Under thy protecting mantle,
    Queen belov'd, I fly;
There I wish to live securely,
    There I hope to die.

If I chance my life to finish,
    Mary, loving thee,
Then I also know, dear Lady,
    Heaven is for me.

Cast thy gentle bonds around me,
    And my heart enchain,
Prisoner of love for ever
    Safe will I remain.

Thus my heart, O sweetest Mary,
    Is not mine, but thine:
Take it; give it all to Jesus,
    Ne'er shall it be mine.

14.   *Mary, Virgin of virgins.*

Of all virgins thou art fairest,
    Dearest Mary, Heavenly Queen;
Of all creatures thou art purest,
    Like to thee was never seen.

Thy sweet face is like the heavens,
    Full of grace and purity;
Beauty so divine adorns it,
    God alone surpasses thee!

Thy bright eyes with love are beaming,
    Like twin stars of heaven they shine;
And thy looks are flaming arrows,
    Wounding hearts with love divine.

Thy chaste hands, whose sight enamours,
    Are like pearls of lustre rare;
Ever full of heavenly treasures,
    For all those who ask a share.

Queen art thou, whom all things worship,
    Earth and hell, and heaven above;
But thy heart o'erflows with goodness,
    Just and sinners feel thy love.

When, ah, when, at length in heaven,
    May I hope thy face to see?
When, ah, when?—my heart keeps sighing—
    Haste—I faint—I pine for thee!

Souls unnumber'd thou dost ever
    Rescue from the Evil One:
Dearest Lady, grant me also
    Not to lose thy blessed Son.

Him who gave us such a Mother
    Let our grateful songs proclaim;
Loving hearts and joyful voices
    Praise her great Creator's name!

Glory to the name of Mary!
    Raise your voices—louder raise!
And of Jesus, Son of Mary,
    Every creature chant the praise!

15.   Aspirations to Mary.

Knowest thou, sweet Mary,
    Whereto I aspire?
'Tis my hope to love thee,—
    This is my desire.

I would e'er be near thee,
    Queen most fair and sweet!
Do not, do not drive me
    From my Mother's feet!

Then, O Rose most lovely!
    Let me hear from thee,
Loving Mother! tell me
    What thou wilt of me.

More I cannot offer,
    Lo! I bring my heart;
Lovingly I give it,
    Ne'er from thee to part.

Lady, thou didst take it,
    'Tis no longer mine:
Long since thou didst love it,
    And its love was thine!

DEVOTIONAL.

> Do not, then, forsake me,
> Mother of sweet Love,
> Till one day thou see me
> Safe in heaven above.

---

16.   *Our Mother, Mary.*

> Thou art clement, thou art chaste,
> Mary, thou art fair;
> Of all mothers sweetest, best,
> None with thee compare.

> O Mother blest! whom God bestows
> On sinners and on just,
> What joy, what hope, thou givest those
> Who in thy mercy trust!
>   Thou art clement, &c.

> O Heavenly Mother! Mistress sweet!
> It never yet was told
> That suppliant sinner left thy feet
> Unpitied, unconsoled.
>   Thou art clement, &c.

O Mother pitiful and mild!
  Cease not to pray for me;
For I do love thee as a child,
  And sigh for love of thee.
        Thou art clement, &c.

Most pow'rful Mother! all men know
  Thy Son denies thee nought;
Thou askest—wishest it—and, lo,
  His power thy will has wrought.
        Thou art clement, &c.

Mother of Love! for me obtain,
  Ungrateful though I be,
To love that God who first could deign
  To show such love to me.
        Thou art clement, &c.

---

17. **Mary, the Mother of Mercy.**

Look down, O Mother Mary!
  From thy bright throne above;
Cast down upon thy children
  One only glance of love.

DEVOTIONAL.

And if a heart so tender
   With pity flows not o'er,
Then turn away, O Mother!
   And look on us no more.

See how, ungrateful sinners,
   We stand before thy Son;
His loving heart upbraids us
   The evil we have done.

But if thou wilt appease Him,
   Speak for us,—but one word;
Thou only canst obtain us
   The pardon of our Lord.

O Mary, dearest Mother!
   If thou wouldst have us live,
Say that we are thy children,
   And Jesus will forgive.

Our sins make us unworthy
   That title still to bear;
But thou art still our Mother,
   Then show a Mother's care.

THE BLESSED VIRGIN MARY.

Open to us thy mantle;
　There stay we without fear:
What evil can befall us
　If, Mother, thou art near?

O sweetest, dearest Mother!
　Thy sinful children save;
Look down on us with pity,
　Who thy protection crave.

---

18. *The Name of Mary.*

Mother Mary, Queen most sweet!
　Joy and love my heart inflame;
Gladly shall my lips repeat
　Every moment thy dear name.

Ah! that name, to God so dear,
　Has my heart and soul enslaved;
Like a seal it shall appear
　Deep on heart and soul engraved.

When the morning gilds the skies,
　I will call on Mary's name;
When at evening twilight dies,
　Mary, still will I exclaim.

Sweetest Mary, bend thine ear:
    Thou my own dear mother art;
Therefore shall thy name so dear
    Never from my lips depart.

If my soul is sore oppress'd
    By a load of anxious care,
Peace once more will fill my breast
    When thy name reëchoes there.

Waves of doubt disturb my peace,
    And my heart is faint with fear;
At thy name the billows cease,
    All my terrors disappear.

When the demon hosts invade,—
    When temptation rages high,
Crying, "Mary, Mother! aid!"
    I will make the tempter fly.

This shall be my comfort sweet,
    When the hand of death is nigh,
Mary! Mary! to repeat
    Once again,—and then, to die.

19. On the Loveliness of Mary.

Raise your voices, vales and mountains,
Flow'ry meadows, streams, and fountains,
   Praise, oh, praise the loveliest Maiden
     Ever the Creator made.

Murm'ring brooks, your tribute bringing,
Little birds with joyful singing,
   Come with mirthful praises laden;
     To your Queen be homage paid.

Say, sweet Virgin, we implore thee,
Say what beauty God sheds o'r thee;
   Praise and thanks to Him be given,
     Who in love created thee.

Like a sun with splendour glowing
Gleams thy heart with love o'erflowing;
   Like the moon in starry heaven
     Shines thy peerless purity.

Like the rose and lily blooming,
Sweetly heaven and earth perfuming,
   Stainless, spotless, thou appearest,
     Queenly beauty graces thee.

But to God, in whom thou livest,
Sweeter joy and praise thou givest,
   When to Him in beauty nearest,
   Yet so humble thou canst be.

Lovely Maid! to God most pleasing,
And for us His wrath appeasing,
   Oh! by all thy love for Jesus,
   Show to us thy clemency.

---

20. A Soul the Lover of Mary.

I AM the lover of a Queen,
   Whose heart so sweet and kind doth prove,
   That seeing one who seeks her love,
She scouts him not though poor and mean.

She sits a Queen, with heavenly grace;
   But from her throne her gentle eyes
   Look down on him who humbly sighs
To see the beauty of her face.

This Virgin is so pure, that she
   Was chosen by the Eternal Word
   The Spouse, the Mother of our Lord;
And she has stol'n my heart from me.

Oh! could I but behold, one day,
  All hearts with love of her inflam'd,
  And hear her sweetest name proclaim'd
By every tongue in joyful lay!

Then in sweet harmony should flow,
  In every land through endless days:
  Praise be to Mary, ceaseless praise!
And praise to God who loved her so!

Let him who wills seek other love,
  If earthly beauty can rejoice
  His soul:—she only is my choice
Whose beauty ravished God above.

Then, Mary, stretch thy hand to me,
  Sweet loving Robber! seize thy prey:
  Take from my breast this heart away,
Which sighs and languishes for thee.

That fire of love into it pour
  With which thou ceasest not to burn,
  That my poor heart, like thine, may yearn
With love of Jesus evermore.

21. The Madonna's Lullaby.

Mary sings, the ravish'd heavens
    Hush the music of their spheres;
Soft her voice, her beauty fairer
    Than the glancing stars appears:
While to Jesus, slumbering nigh,
Thus she sings her lullaby:

"Sleep, my Babe, my God, my Treasure,
    Gently sleep: but, ah! the sight
With its beauty so transports me,
    I am dying of delight:
Thou canst not Thy Mother see,
Yet Thou breathest flames to me.

"If within your lids unfolded,
    Slumbering eyes, you seem so fair;
When upon my gaze you open,
    How shall I your beauty bear?
Ah! I tremble when you wake,
Lest my heart with love should break.

"Cheeks than sweetest roses sweeter,
    Mouth where lurks a smile divine,—

Though the kiss my Babe should waken,
  I must press those lips to mine.
Pardon, Dearest, if I say
Mother's love will take no nay.'

As she ceased, the gentle Virgin
    Clasped the Infant to her breast,
And, upon His radiant forehead
    Many a loving kiss impress'd:
Jesus woke, and on her face
Fixed a look of heavenly grace.

Ah! that look, those eyes, that beauty,
    How they pierce the Mother's heart!
Shafts of love from every feature
    Through her gentle bosom dart.
Heart of stone! can I behold
Mary's love, and still be cold?

Where, my soul, thy sense, thy reason?
    When will these delays be o'er?
All things else, how fair so ever,
    Are but smoke: resist no more!
Yes! 'tis done! I yield my arms
Captive to those double charms.

If, alas, O heavenly beauty!
   Now so late those charms I learn,
Now at least, and ever, ever
   With thy love my heart will burn,
For the Mother and the Child,
Rose and Lily undefiled.

Plant and fruit, and fruit and blossom,
   I am theirs, and they are mine;
For no other prize I labour,
   For no other bliss I pine;
Love can every pain requite,
Love alone is full delight.

---

22.   The Mother of Sorrows.

"O vos omnes qui transitis per viam, attendite, et videte si est dolor sicut dolor meus."

"O all ye that pass by the way attend, and see if there be any sorrow like to my sorrow." *Lamentations*, L 12.

O YE who pass along the way
   All joyous, where with grief I pine,
In pity pause awhile, and say,
   Was ever sorrow like to mine.

See, hanging here before my eyes,
  This body, bloodless, brais'd, and torn,—
Alas! it is my Son who dies,
  Of love deserving, not of scorn.

For know, this weak and dying man
  Is Son of Him who made the earth,
And me, before the world began,
  He chose to give Him human birth.

He is my God! and since that night
  When first I saw His infant grace,
My soul has feasted on the light,
  The beauty of that heavenly face.

For He had chosen me to be
  The lov'd companion of His heart;
And ah! how that dear company
  With love transpierc'd me like a dart!

And now behold this loving Son
  Is dying in a woe so great,
The very stones are moved to moan
  In sorrow at His piteous state.

Where'er His failing eyes are bent,
    A friend to help He seeks in vain;
All, all on vengeance are intent,
    And eager to increase His pain.

Eternal Father! God of Love!
    Behold thy Son! ah! see His woe!
Canst Thou look down from heaven above,
    And for Thy Son no pity show?

But, no—that Father sees His Son
    Cloth'd with the sins of guilty men;
And spares not that Belovèd One,
    Though dying on His cross of pain.

My Son! my Son! could I at least
    Console Thee in this hour of death,
Could I but lay Thee on my breast,
    And there receive Thy parting breath!

Alas! no comfort I impart;
    Nay, rather this my vain regret
But rends still more Thy loving heart,
    And makes Thy death more bitter yet.

THE BLESSED VIRGIN MARY.

Ah, loving souls! love, love that God
    Who all inflamed with love expires;
On you His life He has bestowed;
    Your love is all that He desires.

---

23.   *The Death of Mary.*

UPLIFT the voice and sing
    The Daughter and the Spouse,
The Mother of the King,
    To whom creation bows!

    Praise to Mary, endless praise!
        Raise your joyful voices, raise!
    Praise to God who reigns above,
        Who has made her for His love

When Mary lingered yet
    An exile from her Son,
Like fairest lily, set
    'Mid thorns of earth alone,
        Praise to Mary, &c

F.

To be with God on high,
    Her heart was all on fire;
She sought and asked to die,
    With humble sweet desire.
          Praise to Mary, &c.

At length her Heavenly Spouse,
    Who loved her with such love,
Invites her to repose
    With Him in heaven above.
          Praise to Mary, &c.

She waits till death appear,
    And let her spirit go;
But death approached with fear,
    And dared not strike the blow.
          Praise to Mary, &c.

Then came sweet Love from heaven,
    And with his flaming dart
The mortal wound was given
    To Mary's stainless heart.
          Praise to Mary, &c.

Pierc'd by the deadly wound,
    She gently bowed her head;
Pining with love she swoon'd,
    And, lo, her spirit fled.
          Praise to Mary, &c.

Then did that beauteous Dove
    Spring joyfully on high;
Her Son receives with love,
    And bears her to the sky.
          Praise to Mary, &c.

And now, bright Queen of Love!
    While seated on thy throne,
High in the realms above,
    Near to thy glorious Son,
          Praise to Mary, &c.

Hear, from that blest abode,
    A sinner cries to thee:
Teach me to love that God
    Who bears such love to me.
          Praise to Mary, &c.

24. The Assumption of Mary.

Fly, my soul, with Mary fly,
Soar beyond the golden sky,
Mount to Mary's throne on high.

Bright the queenly crown she won,
Sweet the reign she has begun,
As she stands beside her Son.
     Fly, my soul, &c.

How endure this long delay?
Living here, how can I stay
From such beauty far away?
     Fly, my soul, &c.

Sad my lot is here below;
Who can hope or life bestow?
Who will help or pity show?
     Fly, my soul, &c.

But, though far away from me,
Still our sovereign Queen will be
Full of love and clemency.
     Fly, my soul, &c.

THE BLESSED VIRGIN MARY.

With a mother's loving care
She will lift those hands so fair,
And will save us by her prayer.
              Fly, my soul, &c.

Mother's heart can ne'er forget
That we are her children yet,
By such dangers fierce beset.
              Fly, my soul, &c.

Gently, still, she bends her eyes
On the soul that longs and sighs
For her love, the heavenly prize.
              Fly, my soul, &c.

Blest that soul who, like the dove,
Borne upon the wings of love,
Follows her to heaven above.
              Fly, my soul, &c.

25. Invocation of the Blessed Virgin Mary in time of Temptation.

Haste, my Mother, run to help me;
    Mother, haste, do not delay;
See from hell the envious serpent
    Comes my trembling soul to slay.

Ah! his very look affrights me,
    And his cruel rage I fear;
Whither fly, if he attacks me?
    See him, see him coming near!

Lo! I faint away with terror,
    For if yet thou dost delay,
He will dart at me his venom;
    Then, alas! I am his prey.

Cries and tears have nought availed me,
    Spite of all I see him there;
Saints I call till I am weary,
    Still he stands with threat'ning air.

THE BLESSED VIRGIN MARY.

Now his mighty jaws are open,
    And his forkèd tongue I see;
Ah! he coils to spring upon me,—
    Mother! hasten, make him flee.

Mary! yes, the name of Mary
    Strikes with dread my cruel foe;
Straight he flees, as from the sunbeam
    Swiftly melts the winter's snow.

Now he's gone; but do thou ever
    Stay beside me, Mother dear;
Then the hellish fiend to tempt me
    Never more will venture near.

Part Second.

ASCETICAL.

---

26.   *On the Tomb of Alexander the Great.*

Behold the end of all the pomp of earth,—
All human greatness, beauty, noble birth !—
Worms, rottenness, a little dust, a stone,
Close the brief scene of life for ev'ry one.
Who gives his heart to God alone is wise,
Dead to the world already ere he dies.
O thou that readest this ! thou, too, one day
Must die;—which lot dost thou prefer, I pray,
To die a slave, and then in bliss to reign,—
Or die a king, and pass to endless pain ?
Reflect, prepare; the present time flies fast;
Repentance comes too late when life is past.

---

27. Eternal Maxims.

Why serve the world, thy enemy,
    And from thy thankless heart dethrone
That God whose love created thee
    To love and serve Himself alone?

Slave of a tyrant thou dost live;
    He promises, and breaks his word,
And for thy service nought can give
    But bitter thorns as thy reward.

Remember, death will come one day;
    His touch thy fragile life destroys;
Then, then, alas! will fade away
    Earth's cheating hopes and empty joys.

All worldly pleasures then will be
    To thee but weariness and woe;
The scene of life must close for thee,
    Thy part is played, and thou must go.

That body thou hast oft caress'd
    Such noisome stench shall send around,
That all will fly the loathsome pest,
    And hide the carrion in the ground.

Forth flies the spirit from this clay,
    Alone before its God to stand;
The soul scarce yet has passed away,
    The judge already is at hand.

Sinner! sinner! what wilt thou do,
    Standing before the awful throne?
In vain for mercy wouldst thou sue,—
    Stern Justice triumphs there alone.

Ah! miserable, thoughtless one!
    Say, what excuse thou darest bring
Before that gaze of brightest sun,
    The face of thy offended King.

What horror then the soul shall pierce,
    When, spurned away by heavenly ire,
'Tis hurled into the torment fierce
    Of never, never-ending fire!

Then shall be closed upon thy pain
    The gates of hope and liberty;
Thou seekest death,—in vain, in vain;
    It flies, and mocks thy misery.

That moment when this life shall fail,
    Or heaven or hell thy lot must be;
Eternal joys or endless wail,—
    O moment! O eternity!

Think, then, ere yet this life is o'er,
    On that whereon thy ALL depends;
That EVERMORE or NEVERMORE,
    Eternity which never ends!

---

28. **Stanzas for the Evening Exhortations at a Mission.**

"*Per li sentimenti di notte.*"*

'Tis the Lord hath sent me hither,
    Messenger of pardon free;
Day of grace and hour of mercy,
    Grace perhaps the last for thee!

---

* It was the practice of St. Alphonso in his missions to send some of the missionaries, accompanied by clerics with a cross and lighted torches, to make short exhortations at the corners of the streets and public places for the first few evenings of the mission. The object of these exhortations was to excite the people to penance, and invite them to

ASCETICAL.

Lo! a God of all compassion
  Calls thee; shall He call in vain?
If thou yet reject His mercy,
  Will He ever call again?

Sinner, thou art foe of Heaven,
  And thou tremblest not with fear?
Cease those sins, my child, ah! leave them;
  Death advances, hell is near!

Now thy Lord is waiting, waiting;
  But He will not always wait:
When the day of vengeance breaketh,
  Cries for mercy come too late.

Turn to God in humble penance,
  Sinner, do not still delay;
Do not scorn the love of Jesus,
  Cast His mercy not away.

attend the exercises of the mission. A stanza of some suitable hymn was first sung, and then the missionary gave a short but animated exhortation. The stanzas here translated are given in the works of St. Alphonso to serve for these occasions, and became, as it were, the text of the succeeding exhortation.

Lost in sin, and yet rejoicing!
  Far from God, and canst thou sleep?
On the brink of fell damnation,
  And thou carest not to weep?

Soon thy life will end, poor sinner,—
  Know'st thou *when* the end will be?
Who can tell? perhaps, my brother,
  Death *this night* will come *to thee*.

Think of death!—that awful moment
  When thy dream of life must end;
Boundless bliss or ceaseless torments
  On that moment, death, depend.

Live thy life of sinful pleasures,
  Sinner, yet *the end must come!*
Then, bold man, thy outraged Saviour
  Shall be Judge to seal thy doom

Whither shalt thou fly for refuge
  From that justly angered One,
Sinner, when He shall reproach thee
  All the evil thou hast done?

Souls to hell are blindly running,
    Ah! what myriads who can tell?
On they go, because they *think not*
    What a fearful thing is *hell!*

---

29.   Act of Contrition.

I HAVE offended Thee, my God,
    Alas! my dearest Lord;
Thou Sea of Goodness Infinite,
    And Fount of Love adored.

Ungratefully, without a cause,
    I have offended Thee,
Who on the cross to give me life
    Didst die through love for me.

But I am sorry, O my God!
    In mercy, Lord, forgive;
I never will offend Thee more,—
    No, never while I live.

May every moment of my life
    Be spent in bitter tears,
To mourn my past ingratitude,
    The sins of former years!

30. Invitation to Solitude.

"I will lead her into solitude, and I will speak to her heart." Osee, ii. 14.

Fly hither from the storm that rages round;
Fly, where true peace in solitude is found;
Where cares and strife and worldly troubles
    cease,
Here I invite thee to repose in peace.
A gift awaits thee here: My light divine,
To loving souls so dear, on thee shall shine;
Here thou shalt see how vile is all the earth,
How sweet My love to those who know its
    worth.

Then from My lips that sweet inviting word,
That bids thee love Me, shall by thee be heard;
How much I always loved thee thou shalt see,
And how ungrateful thou hast been to Me.
Sweet contrite tears thy wounds of sin shall
    heal,
The ardour of My love thou then shalt feel.
And here I wait thee to bestow in love
A foretaste of the joys of heaven above.

31. To the Holy Ghost. The Soul all for God.

Begone, ye vain hopes, ye attachments of earth;
   Give your joys to such souls as no higher
       can soar;
Away, far away from my mem'ry begone,
   For I seek you no longer, esteem you no
       more;
O God of my heart! make me love Thee alone.

Adieu, every creature; I leave you with joy;
   I no longer am yours, nay, I am not my own:
I belong but to God, from all else I am free;
   I am Thine, dearest Jesus,—all Thine,—
       Thine alone;
My best-beloved Good! let me cling but to Thee.

O amiable Lord! let Thy sweet holy love
   Now possess my whole being and reign
       over me;
Let Thy love in my heart every passion restrain;
   In that heart which was once so rebellious
       to Thee,
O amiable Lord! come, establish Thy reign.

O Heavenly Dew! that so sweetly dost fall,
    Of passions unholy Thou calmest the glow;
Ah! make me for ever enamour'd of Thee,
    And live to seek only my God here below.
O Heavenly Dew! descend gently on me.

O Fire all Divine! who with heavenly flames
    Dost those souls where Thou glowest make
        holy and blest,
Come Thou to my heart, make it worthy to burn
    With Thy holiest ardours; inflame Thou
        my breast;
O Fire all Divine! for Thy ardours I yearn.

O Infinite Love! Ah, how blessèd is he
    Who beholds Thy sweet face there in heaven above!
Oh! when shall I too come Thy beauty to see,
    And enjoy Thee for ever in transports of love?
O Infinite Love! haste to draw me to Thee.

32.   *Sighs of Love to Jesus Christ.*
The Soul that gives itself all to Jesus.

World, thou art no more for me;
World, I am no more for thee;—
All affections, dear or sweet,
All are laid at Jesus' feet.

He has so enamoured me
Of His heavenly charity,
That no earthly goods inspire
Aught of love or vain desire.

Jesus, Love, be Thou my own;
Thee I long for,—Thee alone;
All myself I give to Thee,
Do whate'er Thou wilt with me.

Life without Thy love would be
Death, O Sovereign Good! to me.
Bound and held by Thy dear chains
Captive now my heart remains.

O my Life! my soul from Thee
Can henceforth no longer flee;
By Thy loving arrow slain,
Now Thy prey it must remain.

If ungrateful worms like me
Merit not the love of Thee,
Thou, sweet Lord, hast well deserved
To be ever loved and served.

Then, O God, my heart inflame;
Give that love which Thou dost claim;
Payment I will ask for none,
Love demands but love alone.

God of Beauty, Lord of Light!
Thy good will is my delight;
Now henceforth Thy will divine
Ever shall in all be mine.

Come, O Jesus, I implore,
Pierce Thy heart, 'tis mine no more;
Kindle in my breast Thy fire,
That of love I may expire.

Ah! my Spouse, I love but Thee;
Thou my Love shalt ever be;
Thee I love; I love and sigh
For Thy love one day to die.

33. How amiable is the Will of God!

'Tis Thy good pleasure, not my own,
In Thee, my God, I love alone;
And nothing I desire of Thee
But what Thy goodness wills for me.
   O will of God! O will Divine!
   All, all our love be ever Thine.

In love no rival canst Thou bear,
But Thou art full of tenderest care;
And fire and sweetness all divine
To hearts which once are wholly Thine.
              O will of God, &c.

In Thee all pure affections live,
To love Thou dost perfection give;
While ever burning with desires
The loving soul to Thee aspires.
              O will of God, &c.

Thou makest crosses soft and light,
And death itself seem sweet and bright:

No cross nor fear that soul dismays
Whose will to Thee united stays.
    O will of God, &c.

To all the glorious choirs of heaven
Their very bliss by Thee is given;
And heaven itself deprived of Thee
Would be a land of misery.
    O will of God, &c.

Yea, to the lost who burn in hell,
If in their souls Thy love could dwell,
The very flames and torments there
Would seem but sweet and light to bear.
    O will of God, &c.

Oh! that one day my life may end
In closest bonds to Thee enchained!
For thus to die is not to die,
But live, and live eternally.
    O will of God, &c.

To Thee I consecrate and give
My heart and being while I live;

ASCETICAL.

Jesus, Thy heart alone shall be
My love for all eternity.
    O will of God, &c.

Alike in pleasure and in pain
To please Thee is my joy and gain;
That, O my Love, which pleases Thee
Shall evermore seem best to me.
  May heaven and earth with love fulfil,
  My God, Thy ever-blessed will!

---

34. On the Love which Jesus bears to the Soul.

OH, it were joy and high reward,
  Transpierc'd with wound of love, to die
For that most lovely, loving God,
  For whom alone all hearts should sigh.

Such is His beauty, such His grace,
  That stars of heaven, or gems of earth,
Compared with that divinest face
  Lose all their loveliness and worth.

He seeks His prey with skill divine,
    He draws His bow, the arrow flies,
The heart is pierced, and forced to pine
    With love for Him for whom it dies.

To wound those souls He longs to gain,
    The charm of varied guise He found,
And all to make those hearts remain
    Close to His heart for ever bound.

For this the Word Divine appears
    On earth, a babe, so poor, so weak;
And from our hearts, with infant tears,
    All love, He came our love to seek.

In youth He next is seen again
    A lowly humble artisan,
And God's own Son does not disdain
    The vilest services of man.

At last a criminal in chains
    Himself unto His spouse He shows;
And thus His life of varied pains
    He ends amid the direst woes.

His love does more;—in form of bread
    To give Himself He yet desires;
There with Himself the soul is fed
    That loves, and to His love aspires.

His love knows every winning way;
    He spares no toil, He fears no pain,
To make another heart His prey,
    Or truer love from it to gain.

Sometimes He loves to banish fear,
    With all the sweetness of a spouse;
Anon He shows a look severe:
    'Tis all fresh fervour to arouse.

Of old He deigned my heart to woo,
    And bound me with love's fiery chains;
Then seized my heart His hostage true,
    And jealous still His prey retains.

Then silence, wicked world! depart,—
    Seek not esteem or love of mine;
Another Lover owns my heart,
    His charms are other far than thine.

35. Hymn to God the Creator.

Why didst Thou not create my soul
   From all eternity,
Since from eternity, dear Lord!
   Thou always lovedst me?

For then to Thee a grateful love
   My heart could have returned
From that first moment when unsought
   Thy love for me thus burned.

I pine not now for the delights
   Of Paradise above,
But only to behold Thy face,
   And gaze on Thee with love.

I long to be for ever fixed
   In that blest changeless state,
Where I might love Thee with a love
   Immeasurably great.

I look around,—amazed, I cry,
   Is it, alas! for this—
This lump of earth, this ant-hill vile,
   Men lose eternal bliss?

To suffer or to die, my soul!
    For if thou canst not gain
The battle to be fought on earth,
    In heaven thou canst not reign.

God sees me—and He is my Judge;
    The sentence, Heaven or Hell;
And there where'er my doom decides,
    For ever shall I dwell.

36.   The Soul sighing for God.

THIS heart of mine is sighing,
    And yet I know not why;
Its sighs with love are laden,
    But whither do they fly?

My trembling heart, oh, tell me,
    Wherefore these burning sighs?
"I sigh for God, I languish
    For Jesus," it replies.

Sigh on, my heart, and cease not
    With sighs of love to swell;
Spend all thy life in loving
    Him who loves thee so well.

Sigh on, and let thy Jesus
    Alone possess thy breast,
And all thy hope in Mary
    With childlike spirit rest.

Send forth thy sighs like arrows
    To wound thy conqu'ror's heart,
Then hope for gifts the choicest
    His goodness can impart.

My trembling sighs, ah, hasten,
    To Jesus haste away;
Then at His feet take refuge,
    And there for ever stay.

Say, that a heart all burning
    With love, has sent you there;
And ask what it shall bid you,
    For He will grant its prayer.

To love with all its being
    Is all the gift it sues:
Ask,—for to one that loves Him
    No prayer can God refuse.

37. The Soul sighing for Heaven.

Oh! I am dying of desire,
    Sweet Lord, to see thy face;
To linger here on earth I tire,
    O God of Loveliness.
A pang so bitter rends my heart,
I can no more endure the smart;
    Ah! do not, Lord, my grief despise.
I live indeed apart from Thee,
But hope and cry unceasingly,
    O Paradise! O Paradise!

An empty joy, which ends in pain,
    Is all this world bestows;
Deceitful pomp and pageant vain,
    Which death anon will close.
He to whom all save God is nought
Best knows the anguish of the thought—
    I yet might lose my prize;
On thee I fix my longing gaze,
To thee alone my sighs I raise,
    O Paradise! O Paradise!

In vain thou wouldst ensnare my heart
    With wealth and empty joys;
Go, world, thy gifts to those impart
    Who madly love such toys.
Vain pomps, or pleasures stained with sin,
Ah! do not hope my hopes to win,
    For other goods my spirit sighs;—
To reign in heaven I aspire;
This is my hope, this my desire,
    O Paradise! O Paradise!

O beauteous home! where love's reward
    Love will itself bestow;
Where my so sweet and loving Lord
    Himself unveiled will show.
When shall I see that blest abode,
And there behold and love my God?
    When will that wished-for dawn arise?
While now I cry, 'twixt smiles and tears,
Ah, when? ah, when shall end my fears?
    O Paradise! O Paradise!

Part Third.

MYSTICAL.

38. *The Soul enamoured of the Beauty of God.*

Let those who will for other beauties pine,
   God, God alone my love shall ever be;
My God, my Life! O Loveliness divine!
     Whom can I wish to love, and love not
        Thee?

Where could I find a nobler, lovelier heart,
   A heart more worthy object of my love?
Such loveliness, that but to see a part
   Can ravish with delight the saints above.

Ah! foolish souls, that throw away your hearts
   On love of beauties earthly, false, and vain;
Ah! see you not that all true peace departs,
   And leaves within but emptiness and pain?

Love God, love Him, the Beauty infinite,—
   Love God alone, who loveth you so much:
Ah, happy you, if loving Him aright,
     You know the secret ways His heart to touch.

Ye who love God! souls beautiful and chaste!
   Do I not speak the truth? Bear witness, say
What peace, what joy He gives your hearts to taste
     While yet poor exiles here on earth you stay.

Thrice happy now! Ah, then what will you say,
   When once you reach in heaven the home of bliss?
What, when you see unveiled in cloudless day
   Your God, the God of Beauty, as He is?

Alas! could I but live my life again,
   In loving Him should be my sole content:
At least, whate'er of life may yet remain
   Shall all in loving God alone be spent.

Shall it not be, O Loveliness divine?
Then if Thou will it so, give me Thy love;
I seek in vain to give Thee love of mine,
    Unless Thy hand first help me from above.

But more Thou lovest me than I love Thee;
    I seek Thy love, but more Thou seekest mine;
Then Thou belongest even now to me,
    And I shall all and evermore be Thine.

---

39.   The Life of the Spouse.

DESCRIPTION OF THE LIFE OF A SOUL, THE TRUE SPOUSE OF JESUS, FROM THE WORDS OF ST. BERNARD.

"Servus timet, mercenarius sperat, filius honorat; at ego, quia sponsa sum, amo amare, amo amari, amo amorem.

"Exigit Deus timeri ut Dominus, honorari ut Pater, ut Sponsus amari." (*Serm.* 88 *in Cant.*)

The slave fears, the hireling hopes, the son honours; but I, because I am a spouse, love to love, I love to be loved, I love love.

God requires that we fear Him as our Lord, that we honour Him as our Father, that we love Him as our Spouse.

To love is the only true life of a spouse;
    For love, love alone her belovèd she serves;

One dread, and one only, her fears can arouse,
　The dread of not loving Him as He deserves.

To forfeit her treasure, the love of her Lord,
　Were the greatest misfortune she ever could fear:
She seeks no reward—for to love is reward,
　And to love is the hope which her love holds most dear.

But merely to love the dear Spouse of her heart,
　To a soul once espousèd can never give rest;
So, of all that can serve Him, or pleasure impart,
　The spouse who is true ever gives Him the best.

Each action she does, every good she may seek,
　Is to please her dear King and her fealty to prove;
To the heart of a spouse her best love seems but weak;
　When she loves Him the most, then she longs most to love.

How great is the joy such a Spouse must impart,
  When the light of His presence shines clear in her breast!
But when He withdraws, then her desolate heart
  Is pining in darkness, and cannot find rest.

She watches her heart, lest some creature should steal
  A share of that love which to Him is all due;
For she well knows how jealous her Jesus can feel
  Of the love of a spouse who has sworn to be true.

Wherever He leads, the spouse follows Him still;
  He speaks, and the spouse ever faithful obeys;
And such is her pleasure in doing His will,
  That obedience alone is the joy of her days.

She seeks not for pleasures, no wishes has she,
  No will of her own does she take for her
      guide;
For the will of her Spouse the sole pleasure
      must be
  Of a soul that is chosen by Christ for His
      bride.

Since to suffer with joy every pain here below
  Is the best proof of love, while on earth we
      remain,
The spouse who desires her affection to show
  Seeks only and always for suff'ring and pain.

She esteems not their lot whom the worldly
      call great,
  'Tis compassion, not envy, she feels in her
      breast;
But she envies their happy and glorious fate
  Who, united to Jesus, can love Him the best.

When she thinks of the spouses departed in
      peace,
  Who yet are detained in the prison of pain,

She labours with joy for their speedy release,
    That in heaven with God these dear spouses
        may reign.

She would that all hearts, who yet dwell here
        below,
    With the love of her Spouse should so
        ardently burn,
That as much as He merits, so each heart
        should glow,
    Or at least with such love as that heart can
        return.

And when she sees others offend her Belov'd,
    Oh! for them with what fervour she pleads
        at His feet,
That hearts so rebellious and proud may be
        moved,
    And return to the love of a Saviour so sweet!

Far more does she weep when she sees her own
        heart
    Unfaithful sometimes to the love of her
        Lord;

She welcomes His scourges, she dreads not
    their smart,
  But she weeps for displeasing her Saviour
    adored.

O worldlings! souls made for a kingdom above!
  From that world which deceives you, for
    ever depart;
Be foolish no longer;—give Him all your love,
  Who only and ever brings peace to the
    heart.

No spouse will I own but my Saviour and
    King:
  Yet it is not the glory I seek, nor the name;
'Tis the faith and the love of a spouse I would
    bring,
  And that faith and that love my whole life
    shall proclaim.

And since my sweet Jesus in heaven bestows
    Himself as a spouse to the spouse of His
    love,
Here I long but to suffer, I ask not repose;
  I await my repose there, in heaven above.

MYSTICAL.

40. Aspirations to Jesus.

Jesus, my sweetest Lord!
Jesus, my sweetest Lord!
My Good, my Spouse adored!

My God, O Goodness Infinite,
  My life's true Life art Thou;
Flame of my heart, my Spouse most sweet,
  My love to Thee I vow.
      Jesus, my sweetest Lord, &c.

Jesus, for Thee I pine away,
  My love, and my desire;
And, more enamoured day by day,
  I burn with heavenly fire.
      Jesus, my sweetest Lord, &c.

Ah, Jesus, I would ever weep
  That I offended Thee;
Mine was ingratitude too deep,
  And basest treachery.
      Jesus, my sweetest Lord, &c.

My Jesus, when I call to mind
  That such a wretch as I

Have crucified a God so kind,
   I fain of grief would die.
          Jesus, my sweetest Lord, &c.

O Thou my Hope, make me remain
   Faithful for evermore:
Better to die than be again
   As I have been before.
          Jesus, my sweetest Lord, &c.

While night and day my foes allure,
   In Thee do I confide:
Take Thou and place my heart secure
   Within Thy piercèd side.
          Jesus, my sweetest Lord, &c.

With Thy sweet chains, O Jesus, bind
   My rebel heart to Thee;
Till death, my safety I will find
   In such captivity.
          Jesus, my sweetest Lord!
          Jesus, my sweetest Lord!
          My Good, my Spouse adored!

MYSTICAL.

41. **Dialogue between Jesus and the Loving Soul.**
(Taken from the " Canticles.")

Aperi mihi, soror mea (Cant. v. 2).
Open to Me, My sister.

THE DIVINE SPOUSE.

OPEN to Me, My sister,
   Open to Me thy heart;
My love can bear no longer
   To live from thee apart.

To Me thou art all coldness,
   Yet still for thee I burn;
Ah! see how much I love thee,
   And love for love return.

Anima mea liquefacta est, ut dilectus locutus est (v. 6).
My soul melted when my Beloved spoke.

THE SOUL.

As soon as my Belovèd
   Had made me hear His voice,
Within my breast all melting,
   I felt my heart rejoice.

But oh! what tongue could utter
   The gladness I had known,

Had He but deigned to tarry,
And speak with me alone!

Adjuro vos filiæ Jerusalem, si inveneritis dilectum meum, ut nuntietis ei quia amore langueo (v. 8).
I adjure you, O daughters of Jerusalem, if you find my Beloved, that you tell Him that I languish with love.

My sisters, I entreat you,
  If ye perchance have seen
My Love, as ye were wandering
  Amid the woodlands green,

Tell Him, my heart is mourning
  In sadness night and day,
While banished from His presence
  I languish far away.

Dilectus meus candidus et rubicundus, electus ex millibus (v. 10).
My Beloved is white and ruddy, chosen out of thousands.

My sisters, do you ask me
  Who is that lovely One,
Whose winning charms have conquered
  And made my heart His own?

He is that Lord of Glory,
  Whose sweet and lovely face

Is radiant with the beauty
  Of every heavenly grace!

White is my Love, and ruddy,
  And all surpassing fair;
Among a thousand chosen
  None can with Him compare.

Quæsivi, et non inveni illum; vocavi, et non respondit mihi (v. 6).

I sought Him, and found Him not; I called, and He did not answer me.

My Spouse, my Well-belovèd,
  Ah, tell me where Thou art;
Oh, come, and by Thy presence
  Peace to my soul impart.

I seek Thee; dost Thou fly me?
  I call; dost Thou not hear?
I weep; dost Thou not pity?
  My Spouse, why thus severe?

Fuge, dilecte mi, et assimilare capreæ hinnuloque cervorum super montes aromatum (viii. 14).

Flee away, O my Beloved, and be like to the roe and to the young hart upon the mountains of aromatical spices.

But haste away, Belovèd,
  If love thus makes Thee flee,

That I may learn to follow,
    And grow in love for Thee.

Upon the desert mountains
    Hie Thee, my Love, away;
'Tis there I will await Thee,
    Alone with Thee to stay.

Trahe me: post te curremus in odorem unguentorum tuorum (1. 3).
Draw me: we will run after Thee to the odour of Thy ointments.

By the enticing odour
    Of Thy delights so pure,
O sweetest Lord of Heaven,
    To Thee my soul allure.

Then, by Thy love all ravished,
    A captive, chained, but free,
My heart with love united
    Shall joyful run to Thee.

Ego flos campi, et lilium convallium (li. 1).
I am the flower of the field, and the lily of the valleys.

THE DIVINE SPOUSE.

To all Myself I offer,
    Like flow'ret of the field;

To all that seek Me truly
    My beauty is revealed.

Like lily of the valley,
    He only findeth Me
Who seeketh in the shadows
    Of deep humility.

Hortus conclusus, soror mea, sponsa: emissiones tuæ paradisus (iv. 12, 13).
My sister, My spouse, is a garden enclosed: thy plants are a paradise.

And thou, My spouse, a garden
    Most pleasant dost appear,
So fruitful and so lovely,
    And to My heart so dear:

For thou art closed to creatures,—
    Open to Me alone;
I, only I, possess thee,
    And thou art all Mine own.

As from the heavenly gardens
    Thy fruits are sweet to Me;
Those acts of love so tender,
    Which now I draw from thee.

MYSTICAL.

Averte oculos tuos a me, quia ipsi me avolare fecerunt (vi. 4).
Turn away thy eyes from Me; for they have made Me flee away.

> Ah, turn away thine eyes, love,
>   Those tender looks restrain,
> They pierce like darts, they bind Me,
>   And captive I remain.
>
> Long since thine eyes had made Me
>   My throne in heaven resign,
> And come on earth to seek thee,
>   And join My heart to thine.

Veni, columba mea in foraminibus petræ, ostende mihi faciem tuam; sonet vox tua in auribus meis (ii. 13, 14).
Come, my Dove in the clefts of the rocks; show me thy face; let thy voice sound in My ears.

> Come, O My spouse, My dearest,
>   Come, O My chosen dove!
> Within My heart now enter,
>   Take thy repose of love.
>
> Then turn thy face unto Me,
>   And whisper in My ear,
> For thy sweet voice like music
>   To Me was ever dear.

Say to Me thou dost love Me,
 That word will joy impart;
Say thou art happy with Me,
 And thus console My heart.

Fasciculus myrrhæ dilectus meus mihi; inter ubera mea commorabitur (i. 12).
A bundle of myrrh is my Beloved to me: He shall abide between my breasts.

THE SOUL.

If Thee, my Spouse, I love not,
 Who else my heart could woo?
For Thou art all endearing,
 Most lovely and most true.

So sweet to me Thou seemest,
 That ever shalt Thou rest
Like to a fragrant bundle
 Of myrrh upon my breast.

Qui pascitur inter lilia (ii. 16).
Who feedeth among the lilies.

But Thou who ever feedest
 Among the lilies fair,
And 'mid the flowers of virtue
 That bloom with lustre rare,

Come to my heart, and with Thee
    Come ev'ry flower of spring,
As pledge of Thy affection,
    Those flowers Thou lovest bring.

Fortis ut mors dilectio (viii. 6).
Love is strong as death.

As sense and feeling languish
    At the approach of death,
And earthly goods and pleasures
    Fade at his fatal breath;

So Love divine o'er changes
    The soul He makes His own,
And then it finds no pleasure
    In aught but Him alone.

Dura sicut infernus æmulatio; lampades ejus, lampades ignis atque flammarum (viii. 6).
Jealousy is hard as hell; the lamps thereof are fire and flames.

Love is a flame that kindles
    Such ardour in the breast,
As makes it prompt to labour,
    And seek no ease nor rest.

Unconquered still, unwearied,
    It burns with deep desire
To make all hearts, all creatures,
    With love of God on fire.

And as in hell the torment
    Of fire insatiate glows,
So in the ardent lover
    His love unceasing grows.

En ipse stat post parietem nostrum, respiciens per fenestras, &c. Surge, propera, &c. (ii. 9, 10).
Behold, He standeth behind our wall, looking through the windows, looking through the lattices. Behold, my Beloved speaketh to me: arise, make haste, My Love, My Dove, My beautiful One, and come.

Behold the Spouse stands hidden,
    His eyes are fixed on me,
And is my love still burning,
    Or cold, He looks to see.

Hark! the Belovèd speaketh:
    Arise, My Lovely One,
Come to thy throne of glory,
    The storm is past and gone.

Inveni quem diligit anima mea: tenui eum, nec dimittam (III. 4).
I found Him whom my soul loveth: I held Him, and I will not let Him go.

O lot too sweet, too happy!
   O bliss! I now have found
My Spouse, my Love, my Treasure,
   To whom my heart is bound.

Then ever, O Belovèd,
   Mine ever shalt Thou be;
No more, no more, my Treasure,
   Shalt Thou depart from me.

Introduxit me in cellam vinariam (ii. 4).
He brought me into the cellar of wine.

Now to the lonely cellar,
   All full of mystic wine,
The King, my Lover, led me
   With tenderness divine.

What is that mystic cellar?
   Ah! 'tis His Sacred Heart;
And love, the wine entrancing,
   He deigneth to impart.

MYSTICAL.

Surge, aquilo, et veni, auster, perfla hortum meum, et fluant aromata (iv. 16).

Arise, O north wind, and come, O south wind, blow through my garden, and let the aromatical spices thereof flow.

 Ye thoughts of worldly pleasures,
  Ye wintry winds depart,
 And come no more to trouble
  The peace of my poor heart.

 Come, with Thy breath inflaming,
  Spirit of Love Divine!
 Come, fires of love enkindle
  Within this breast of mine:

 For, when Thy heavenly breathings
  Within my garden blow,
 With streams of ev'ry virtue
  My soul shall fragrant flow.

Fulcite me floribus, stipate me malis, quia amore langueo (ii. 5).

Stay me up with flowers; compass me about with apples; because I languish with love.

 Come, O ye heavenward longings!
  Come, sweetest fruits of love!
 Fresh vigour to my spirit
  Bring to me from above.

Within my breast is glowing
    Such sweet, such loving fire,
That lo! my soul is fainting,
    I languish with desire.

Ego dormio, et cor meum vigilat (v. 2).
I sleep, and my heart watcheth.

I sleep, but, ever watchful,
    My heart is loving still
That Sovereign Good, who only
    With joy my heart can fill.

What peaceful sleep, what pleasure,
    What calm repose is this?
No voice of earth intruding,
    Love reigns in silent bliss.

Indica mihi, quem diligit anima mea, ubi pascas, ubi cubes in meridie (i. 6).
Show me, O Thou whom my soul loveth, where Thou feedest, where Thou liest in the mid-day.

Blest spirits, who in heaven
    The sight of God enjoy,
No fear again to lose Him
    Can e'er your bliss destroy.

Ah, when to me my Treasure
    In heaven will you give,
For whom I die of longing,
    For whom alone I live?

Tell me where Thou reposest,
    And with Thy love divine
Vouchsafe to feed, O Jesus,
    This heart so loved by Thine.

O Heaven, in Thy bright palace
    The Spouse His beauty shows,
And all unveiled, there only,
    Himself on all bestows.

Ne suscitetis, neque evigilare faciatis dilectam (iii. 5).
Stir not up, nor awake My beloved.

THE DIVINE SPOUSE.

Ah, see! My spouse now slumbers;
    My loved one do not wake;
That sleep of love entrancing
    Oh, dare not yet to break.

Tranquil she lies, reposing
    In peace of love divine;
Her loving heart united
    In closest bonds to Mine.

MYSTICAL. 101

Quæ est ista, quæ ascendit per desertum, sicut virgula fumi ex aromatibus myrrhæ et thuris, ... deliciis affluens, innixa super dilectum suum? (iii. 6; viii. 5).

Who is she that goeth up by the desert, as a pillar of smoke of aromatical spices of myrrh and frankincense, ... flowing with delights, leaning upon her Beloved?

Before My eyes how charming
   This soul in beauty shone,
Who lived for Me so constant,
   Like turtle-dove alone!

Her heart so true was pining
   With peaceful keen desire,
While love, her prayer inflaming,
   Consumed her in its fire.

Now like a cloud of incense
   Ascending to the skies,
The hearts of all consoling,
   Her fragrant odours rise.

With what delights o'erflowing,
   That soul arises blest,
Who sought with love confiding
   On Me alone to rest!

Vulnerasti cor meum, soror mea, sponsa, in uno oculorum tuorum, et in uno crine colli tui (iv. 9).

Thou hast wounded My heart, My sister, My spouse, with one of thy eyes, and with one hair of thy neck.

    My sister, spouse belovèd,
        Thy dart has pierced Me through;
    Now sweetly I invite thee
        To love thy Lover true.

    This thy desire to please Me
        Has like a fiery dart,
    These thoughts of thine so humble
        Have pierced and won My heart.

Veni de Libano, sponsa mea, veni, coronaberis (iv. 8).

Come from Libanus, My spouse,—come, thou shalt be crowned.

    Oh, come, and quit for ever
        The land of misery,
    Where they who love most truly
        Must suffer most for Me.

    A coronet of roses
        Entwined with lilies chaste,
    The crown of faithful spouses,
        Shall on thy brow be placed.

MYSTICAL.

Pone me ut signaculum super cor tuum (viii. 6).
Put Me as a seal upon thy heart.

   Meanwhile, My spouse, if truly
      Thou bearest in thy breast
   For Me that true affection
      Thou hast so oft expressed,

   Then must thou have My image
      Engraven in thy heart
   By hand of love so deeply
      That never it depart.

   And since thou hast beheld Me
      No shame nor torments fly,
   As spouse I now invite thee
      Upon the cross to die.

---

42. *The Soul introduced into the wine-cellar, and already inebriated with Divine Love.*

   OH! where am I? What cell is this
   In which I breathe an air of bliss,
   So heavenly that I burn and pine,
   Consumed with flames of love divine?

Who led me to this garden fair,
So rich with flowers of beauty rare,
Whose thousand scented breaths impart
A perfume sweet which fills the heart?

A sleep unearthly calms my heart;
Vain creatures, wake me not,—depart!
Ah! leave me, leave me, I entreat,
To sleep yet on, in peace so sweet.

A love all pure embraces me,
And sets my soul's affections free
From earthly things; my heart so blest,
Now finds in God alone its rest.

I burn, and yet no fire is near;
A captive, yet no chains are here;
No dart, yet I am piercèd through;
'Tis past belief, and still 'tis true.

A thousand chains my soul have bound,
A thousand darts my heart have found,
A thousand wounds of love it feels,
The Archer still himself conceals.

Sweet flames of love consume me now,
They death inflict, yet life bestow;
Dying, I live, yet would I not
For lives a thousand change my lot.

Silence and solitude I seek,
And yet of love would ever speak;
I would repose, yet soar above,
And draw with me all hearts to love.

When most alone, 'tis then I see
My best Companion is with me;
And to my Love I most am bound
When most detached from all around.

I seek abasement, yet I reign;
Though leaving all, my All I gain;
I shun all pleasures, yet I find
A joy beyond all joys combined.

I burn, and evermore would burn;
I yearn for God, and still would yearn;
I wish to live, I long to die,—
I know not well for what I sigh!

I seek in vain I know not what;
I love, yet comprehend it not;
Scarce only in my love, I seem
To know I love the Good Supreme.

Come, ye enamoured souls, and say
What comfort can your pain allay,
When sick with love, you feel the smart
Of those sweet flames that burn the heart.

But no one hears, not one replies;
And Thou, my Love, these burning sighs,
These bitter tears which Thou dost see,
But make Thee yet more deaf to me.

Come, Love! for I am now Thy prey;
Who art Thou? and what wilt Thou?—say!
Let me but see Thy beauty nigh,
Then, if Thou wilt, then let me die.

Ah! let me speak, great God above!
Thou knowest all, save how to love;
For Thou art pitiless to me,
A heart that loves and pleases Thee.

If, then, so great Thy love has been,
Why pierce my heart with dart so keen,
And leave me thus in bitter pain,
Apart from Thee to pine in vain?

Ah! Cruel, Cruel One!— but no,
Belovèd!—yes, I call Thee so;
Thou know'st my one, one only thought
Is but to please Thee as I ought.

'Tis love thus leads my tongue astray;
Senseless, I know not what I say:
That piercing dart of charity
Makes me thus mad through love of Thee.

Dear object of my love alone,
Thou one, one only love I own;
My God! my All! O Loveliness!
My Good, my Life, my Happiness!

My Treasure! ah! what can I do,
Thy sweet and noble heart to woo?
Oh, speak, and tell me how I may
Thy love with my poor love repay.

'Twere little in love's fiercest fire
For Thee to languish of desire;
Nor pain nor death could pay the debt;
To be consumed were little yet.

And now, since words can say no more,
Accept, Belovèd, I implore,
This unreserved gift from me,—
All, all I am, I give to Thee.

---

43. The Loving Soul in Desolation.

O DARK and solitary grove,
   Whose sombre shades impart
A gloom that makes thee well accord
   With my sad lonely heart;

Come, bear me friendly company,
   Compassionate my woe,
And suffer thus without restraint
   My sobs and tears to flow.

I weep, and ever still must weep,
    Nought can my tears restrain,
Until my God, my Best-belov'd,
    At length I find again.

Ah! where art Thou, my only Good?
    Ah! whither hast Thou gone?
Far, far away, thus leaving me
    Disconsolate, alone.

Where is that happy time, O God,
    That time of joy and grace,
When the lov'd Spouse consoled my heart
    With His sweet heavenly face;

When, in that sweetest sleep of soul,
    He aimed the flaming dart,
Inflicting first a wound of love,
    Then ravishing my heart;

When, all inflamed with love divine,
    My sighs were breaths of fire;
And while I loved, still more and more
    To love was my desire?

Alas! how soon the cruel storm
    Succeeds that calm so dear;
The very light of heaven above
    Now fills my soul with fear.

Horrors I see and feel around,
    Where'er I look or go;
And every thing inspires with dread,
    And adds fresh pain and woe.

Alas! forsaken and alone
    Myself I ever see,
And in my bitter agony
    No one can comfort me.

Death, death itself with cruel spite
    Torments, but does not kill;
The gates are shut, I cannot flee,
    I live a captive still.

I fain would flee,—but where to find
    A hand to set me free,
If He who life alone can give
    Flies far away from me?

Oh, my Belovèd! help Thou me;
   If Thou hast gone, return;
See how I sigh disconsolate,
   And for Thy presence yearn.

Ah! be at length appeased with me,
   My Life! return again:
And since 'tis Thou hast pierced me thus,
   Heal Thou my hidden pain.

Good cause hast Thou, dear Lord, I own,
   For ever to depart;
Yet see, ah! see, Thy chains remain
   Entwined around my heart.

And should there be, alas! no hope
   Of pardon yet for me,
Still know, dear Jesus, I am Thine,
   And Thine will ever be.

I love Thee, though I seem to be
   But hateful in Thy sight;
And I will ever follow Thee
   Where'er Thou turn Thy flight.

44. In honour of St. Teresa.

On these words of hers: "I am dying because I cannot die."

Ye angels most inflamed
    With fires of heavenly love,
Bright Seraphim! descend
    From your high thrones above;
To this most chosen soul
    Your loving succour bring,
To her, the spouse belov'd
    Of Christ your God and King.

Jesus, your Love, your Life,
    Who loves the pure of heart,
Has pierced Teresa's soul
    With love's own flaming dart,
And lo! she pines away,
    She languishes, she sighs;
For Him who gave the wound
    Of very love she dies.

Too bitter is the pang
    Of such a wounded heart,
That loves and pines away
    From her Belov'd apart.

Come, heavenly spirits, come;
   Console the wounded dove;
Teresa moans with grief
   Of absence from her Love.

To see her loving Spouse
   So fierce is her desire,
That evermore she burns,
   Consuming in its fire.
That sweet and longing wish
   Into His arms to fly,
Is but a living death,
   Because she cannot die.

No angels come to aid;
   Come Thou, who in this breast
Hast kindled flames so dear,
   Come Thou, and give her rest.
Sick is her soul with love,
   And wounded is her heart;
Thou didst inflict the wound,
   Then, Jesus, cure its smart.

Thy spouse was ever true,
   To please thy heart divine,

All earth could give she left,
　　All she could give is Thine;
And now she loves Thee well,
　　And sighs to come to Thee;
She longs to take her flight,—
　　Ah! set her spirit free.

---

45. On the Words of St. Aloysius.

Recede a me, Domine.
Depart from me, O Lord.

Poor heart, what art thou doing? say;
　　Seest not how thy good Master deigns
　　To bind thee with love's strongest chains,
And force thee here with Him to stay?

Where, O my soul, where wilt thou flee?
　　How, thus transfixed with love's keen dart,
　　Canst thou from thy true life depart,
Who on that altar stays for thee?

But ah! my God, what meaneth this?
　　Thou bindest first with such a chain,
　　Then forcest me to go with pain
Away from Thee, my only bliss.

Must I then go?   Yes, I obey;
   But here my heart shall stay with Thee,
   True to thy love still may it be :
I go; then come with me away.

Alas! I cannot tear away
   My soul from Thee, its very life ;
   I start, I wait, in saddest strife ;
I cannot leave, I dare not stay.

Between the two, in doubts and fears,
   I waver still from side to side ;
   While agitated, tost, and tried,
Love's target my poor heart appears.

What strife! what tempest in my will!
   Obedience bids me haste away;
   Thy love then binds and makes me stay,
It ravishes and holds me still.

Thus, when the winds on ocean blow,
   A ship among the billows lost
   By raging storms is fiercely tost,
And dashed with fury to and fro.

With sighs and tears I moan and cry;
   Lov'd Jesus, in Thy mercy sweet,
   From this rude torment, I entreat
Ah! set me free, and let me die.

In heaven, where love alone doth reign,
   There, dearest Jesus, I shall be,
   Close bound, united, tied to Thee,
And never part from Thee again.

Appendix.

VARIOUS HYMNS.

---

46.   *The Sacred Heart of Jesus.*

FLY, my soul, ah, fly away
    To Jesus' heart so kind;
There Love's captive thou shalt stay,
    And truest freedom find.

See, thy foes are all around;
    Thou art pursued, poor thing!
Safety in the ark is found,
    Then thither, dove, take wing.

Why delay? the world is woe,
    And care and cold deceit;
God alone can joy bestow,
    And happiness complete.

APPENDIX.

Give me, Lord, a place to dwell
    Within Thy heart so meek;
This shall be my prison cell,
    Where true repose I seek.

All on earth I now disdain,
    And for Thy love resign;
This the fruit of every pain,
    To bind my heart to Thine.

If within Thy heart divine
    To die my lot should be,
Oh, what happy death were mine!
    Such death were life to me,

---

47.   On the Love of God.
    By MONSIGNORE FALCOJA.

O GOD of loveliness!
    O Lord of Heaven above!
How worthy to possess
    My heart's devoted love!

So sweet Thy countenance,
    So gracious to behold,
That one, one only glance,
    To me were bliss untold.

Thou art blest Three in One,
    Yet undivided still:
Thou art that One alone
    Whose love my heart can fill.
The heavens, the earth below,
    Were fashioned by Thy Word;
How amiable art Thou,
    My ever-dearest Lord!

To think Thou art my God,—
    Oh, thought for ever blest!—
My heart has overflowed
    With joy within my breast.
My soul so full of bliss
    Is plunged as in a sea,
Deep in the sweet abyss
    Of holy charity.

No object here below
    Awakens my desire;

No suffering nor woe
  Can grief or pain inspire.
The world I could despise,
  Though it were all of gold;
Thee only do I prize,
  O mine of wealth untold!

My God, my dearest Love!
  My God for evermore!
My soul's true life above!
  Thee does my heart adore.
No love on earth I own,
  For nought on earth I sigh;
For love of Thee alone
  I faint away, I die.

Were hearts as countless mine
  As sands upon the shore,
All should in choir combine
  To love Thee evermore.
And every heart should yearn
  With tenderest desire,
And in my bosom burn
  With flames of holiest fire.

O Loveliness supreme,
    And Beauty infinite!
O ever-flowing Stream,
    And Ocean of Delight!
O Life by which I live,
    My truest life above,
To Thee alone I give
    My undivided love.

Death even, for Thy sake,
    I count to be no loss;
And sweet repose I take,
    For Thee, on every cross.
Could I but love Thee still
    In the dark pit of hell,
E'en there, to do Thy will,
    I should not fear to dwell.

48.   **To Mary, our Mother.**
               By Mgr. Majello.

When I think o'er my happy lot,
    That, Mary, I am child of thine,
    Then every sorrow, Mother mine,
Swift vanishes and is forgot.

Chos'n Mother of my God to be,
    Thou still art mine own Mother dear;
    What harm then can I ever fear,
Sweet Mary, if thou lovest me?

One only fear can make me sigh,
    'Tis lest I e'er should lose thy love;
    But while my heart shall faithful prove,
Living or dying, blest am I.

Deprived of thee, my lovely Rose,
    Each joy doth bitter grief appear;
    But pain is joy if thou art near,
And death itself is sweet repose.

From Heaven's path he cannot stray
    Who follows thee, his safest guide;

To serve thee and in thee confide,
Is of all good the surest way.

Oh, blest is he whose sole desire
    Is e'er to love thee tenderly;
    Yes, happy he who loveth thee,
And feels his heart with love on fire.

Then grant to me, my sweetest Queen,
    Ever to burn with love of thee,
    Until in heaven I come to see,
Unveil'd, thy loveliness serene.

49. To Mary assumed into Heaven.
By Mgr. Majello.

Mary! thy heart for love
    Alone had ever sighed:
So much it loved, at length
    Of very love it died.

O happy, happy death!
    If death indeed could be,
Blest Virgin! that sweet end
    Which God bestowed on thee.

'Tis in a sweet repose,
    With smile of heavenly mirth,
Thou takest joyful flight
    To Paradise from earth.

Then speed thee, Mother mine,
    Though speeds my life from me;
Haste where thy Son awaits,
    And Heaven welcomes thee.

Oh! that my life could end,
    Sweet Mother, now with thine,
That I might soar to heaven,
    Where all thy glories shine!

Thrice fortunate, my soul,
  Yea, lot supremely blest,
To reach thy Mother's throne,
  And at her feet to rest.

But see, above the choirs
  Of saints and angels bright,
God's Mother near her Son,
  Enthroned in dazzling light.

Come, then, to fetch thy child,
  O Mary, Mother dear!
And tarry by my side
  When my last hour is near.

Yes, this I hope from thee—
  Despise not my request—
To yield my soul in peace
  Upon my Mother's breast!

LONDON:
ROBSON AND LEVEY, PRINTERS, GREAT NEW STREET
FETTER LANE.

www.ingramcontent.com/pod-product-compliance
Lightning Source LLC
Chambersburg PA
CBHW020056170426
43199CB00009B/299